ROBERT BROWNING

1812–1889

ELIZABETH BARRETT BROWNING

1806–1861

ROBERT AND ELIZABETH BROWNING –
AN ANTHOLOGY

ISBN 0–7117–0442–2

*Designed and produced by Parke Sutton Limited, Norwich
for Jarrold Publishing, Norwich*

This selection first published by Jarrold Publishing 1989

Reprinted 1992

Printed in Great Britain 2/92

Contents

This series is respectfully dedicated to
St. John Bosco
(1815–1888)
and
Joanna

Any Wife To Any Husband

I

My love, this is the bitterest, that thou —
Who art all truth, and who dost love me now
    As thine eyes say, as thy voice breaks to say —
Shouldst love so truly, and couldst love me still
A whole long life through, had but love its will,
    Would death that leads me from thee brook delay.

II

I have but to be by thee, and thy hand
Will never let mine go, nor heart withstand
    The beating of my heart to reach its place.
When shall I look for thee and feel thee gone?
When cry for the old comfort and find none?
    Never, I know! Thy soul is in thy face.

III

Oh, I should fade — 'tis willed so! Might I save,
Gladly I would, whatever beauty gave
    Joy to thy sense, for that was precious too.
It is not be to granted. But the soul
Whence the love comes, all ravage leaves that whole;
    Vainly the flesh fades; soul makes all things new.

IV

It would not be because my eye grew dim
Thou couldst not find the love there, thanks to Him
*   Who never is dishonoured in the spark*
He gave us from his fire of fires, and bade
Remember whence it sprang, nor be afraid
*   While that burns on, though all the rest grow dark.*

V

So, how thou wouldst be perfect, white and clean
Outside as inside, soul and soul's demesne
*   Alike, this body given to show it by!*
Oh, three-parts through the worst of life's abyss,
What plaudits from the next world after this,
*   Couldst thou repeat a stroke and gain the sky!*

VI

And is it not the bitterer to think
That, disengage our hands and thou wilt sink
*   Although thy love was love in very deed?*
I know that nature! Pass a festive day,
Thou dost not throw its relic-flower away
*   Nor bid its music's loitering echo speed.*

VII

Thou let'st the stranger's glove lie where it fell;
If old things remain old things all is well,
    For thou art grateful as becomes man best:
And hadst thou only heard me play one tune,
Or viewed me from a window, not so soon
    With thee would such things fade as with the rest.

VIII

I seem to see! We meet and part; 'tis brief;
The book I opened keeps a folded leaf,
    The very chair I sat on, breaks the rank;
That is a portrait of me on the wall —
Three lines, my face comes at so slight a call:
    And for all this, one little hour to thank!

IX

But now, because the hour through years was fixed,
Because our inmost beings met and mixed,
    Because thou once hast loved me — wilt thou dare
Say to thy soul and Who may list beside,
'Therefore she is immortally my bride;
    Chance cannot change my love, nor time impair.

X

'So, what if in the dusk of life that's left,
I, a tired traveller of my sun bereft,
    Look from my path when, mimicking the same,
The fire-fly glimpses past me, come and gone?
— Where was it till the sunset? where anon
    It will be at the sunrise! What's to blame?'

XI

Is it so helpful to thee? Canst thou take
The mimic up, nor, for the true thing's sake,
    Put gently by such efforts at a beam?
Is the remainder of the way so long,
Thou need'st the little solace, thou the strong?
    Watch out thy watch, let weak ones doze and dream!

XII

— Ah, but the fresher faces! 'Is it true,'
Thou'lt ask, 'some eyes are beautiful and new?
    Some hair, — how can one choose but grasp such wealth?
And if a man would press his lips to lips
Fresh as the wilding hedge-rose-cup there slips
    The dew-drop out of, must it be by stealth?

XIII

'It cannot change the love still kept for Her,
More than if such a picture I prefer
*   Passing a day with, to a room's bare side:*
The painted form takes nothing she possessed,
Yet, while the Titian's Venus lies at rest,
*   A man looks. Once more, what is there to chide?'*

XIV

So must I see, from where I sit and watch,
My own self sell myself, my hand attach
*   Its warrant to the very thefts from me —*
Thy singleness of soul that made me proud,
Thy purity of heart I loved aloud,
*   Thy man's-truth I was bold to bid God see!*

XV

Love so, then, if thou wilt! Give all thou canst
Away to the new faces — disentranced,
*   (Say it and think it) obdurate no more:*
Re-issue looks and words from the old mint,
Pass them afresh, no matter whose the print
*   Image and superscription once they bore!*

XVI

Re-coin thyself and give it them to spend, —
It all comes to the same thing at the end,
    Since mine thou wast, mine art and mine shalt be,
Faithful or faithless, sealing up the sum
Or lavish of my treasure, thou must come
    Back to the heart's place here I keep for thee!

XVII

Only, why should it be with stain at all?
Why must I, 'twixt the leaves of coronal,
    Put any kiss of pardon on thy brow?
Why need the other women know so much,
And talk together, 'Such the look and such
    The smile he used to love with, then as now!'

XVIII

Might I die last and show thee! Should I find
Such hardship in the few years left behind,
    If free to take and light my lamp, and go
Into thy tomb, and shut the door and sit,
Seeing thy face on those four sides of it
    The better that they are so blank, I know!

XIX

Why, time was what I wanted, to turn o'er
Within my mind each look, get more and more
    By heart each word, too much to learn at first;
And join thee all the fitter for the pause
'Neath the low doorway's lintel. That were cause
    For lingering, though thou calledst, if I durst!

XX

And yet thou art the nobler of us two:
What dare I dream of, that thou canst not do,
    Outstripping my ten small steps with one stride?
I'll say then, here's a trial and a task —
Is it to bear? — if easy, I'll not ask:
    Though love fail, I can trust on in thy pride.

XXI

Pride? — when those eyes forestall the life behind
The death I have to go through! — when I find,
    Now that I want thy help most, all of thee!
What did I fear? Thy love shall hold me fast
Until the little minute's sleep is past
    And I wake saved. — And yet it will not be!

11

'How They Brought The Good News From Ghent To Aix'

I

I sprang to the stirrup, and Joris, and he;
I galloped, Dirck galloped, we galloped all three;
'Good speed!' cried the watch, as the gatebolts undrew;
'Speed!' echoed the wall to us galloping through;
Behind shut the postern, the lights sank to rest,
And into the midnight we galloped abreast.

II

Not a word to each other; we kept the great pace
Neck by neck, stride by stride, never changing our place;
I turned in my saddle and made its girths tight,
Then shortened each stirrup, and set the pique right,
Rebuckled the cheek-strap, chained slacker the bit,
Nor galloped less steadily Roland a whit.

III

'Twas moonset at starting; but while we drew near
Lokeren, the cocks crew and twilight dawned clear;
At Boom, a great yellow star came out to see;

At Düffield, 'twas morning as plain as could be;
And from Mecheln church-steeple we heard the half-

chime,

So, Joris broke silence with, 'Yet there is time!'

IV

At Aerschot, up leaped of a sudden the sun,
And against him the cattle stood black every one,
To stare thro' the mist at us galloping past,
And I saw my stout galloper Roland at last,
With resolute shoulders, each butting away
The haze, as some bluff river headland its spray:

V

And his low head and crest, just one sharp ear bent back
For my voice, and the other pricked out on his track;
And one eye's black intelligence, — ever that glance
O'er its white edge at me, his own master, askance!
And the thick heavy spume-flakes which aye and anon
His fierce lips shook upwards in galloping on.

VI

By Hasselt, Dirck groaned; and cried Joris, 'Stay spur!
Your Roos galloped bravely, the fault's not in her,
We'll remember at Aix' — for one heard the quick wheeze

Of her chest, saw the stretched neck and staggering knees,
And sunk tail, and horrible heave of the flank,
As down on her haunches she shuddered and sank.

VII

So, we were left galloping, Joris and I,
Past Looz and past Tongres, no cloud in the sky;
The broad sun above laughed a pitiless laugh,
'Neath our feet broke the brittle bright stubble like chaff;
Till over by Dalhem a dome-spire sprang white,
And 'Gallop,' gasped Joris, 'for Aix is in sight!'

VIII

'How they'll greet us!' — and all in a moment his roan
Rolled neck and croup over, lay dead as a stone;
And there was my Roland to bear the whole weight
Of the news which alone could save Aix from her fate,
With his nostrils like pits full of blood to the brim,
And with circles of red for his eye-sockets' rim.

IX

Then I cast loose my buffcoat, each holster let fall,
Shook off both my jack-boots, let go belt and all,
Stood up in the stirrup, leaned, patted his ear,

Called by Roland his pet-name, my horse without peer;
Clapped my hands, laughed and sang, any noise, bad or good,
Till at length into Aix Roland galloped and stood.

X

And all I remember is, friends flocking round
As I sat with his head 'twixt my knees on the ground;
And no voice but was praising this Roland of mine,
As I poured down his throat our last measure of wine,
Which (the burgesses voted by common consent)
Was no more than his due who brought good news from
Ghent.

Love In A Life

I

Room after room,
I hunt the house through
We inhabit together.
Heart, fear nothing, for, heart, thou shalt find her —
Next time, herself! — not the trouble behind her
Left in the curtain, the couch's perfume!
As she brushed it, the cornice-wreath blossomed anew:
Yon looking-glass gleamed at the wave of her feather.

II

Yet the day wears,
And door succeeds door;
I try the fresh fortune —
Range the wide house from wing to the centre.
Still the same chance! she goes out as I enter.
Spend my whole day in the quest, — who cares?
But 'tis twilight, you see, — with such suites to explore,
Such closets to search, such alcoves to importune!

LIFE IN A LOVE

Escape me?
Never —
Beloved!
While I am I, and you are you,
So long as the world contains us both,
Me the loving and you the loth,
While the one eludes, must the other pursue.
My life is a fault at last, I fear:
It seems too much like a fate, indeed!
Though I do my best I shall scarce succeed.
But what if I fail of my purpose here?
It is but to keep the nerves at strain,
To dry one's eyes and laugh at a fall,
And baffled, get up and begin again, —
So the chace takes up one's life, that's all.
While, look but once from your farthest bound
At me so deep in the dust and dark,
No sooner the old hope drops to ground
Than a new one, straight to the self-same mark,
I shape me —
Ever
Removed!

MY LAST DUCHESS

Ferrara

That's my last Duchess painted on the wall,
Looking as if she were alive. I call
That piece a wonder, now: Frà Pandolf's hands
Worked busily a day, and there she stands.
Will't please you sit and look at her? I said
'Frà Pandolf' by design, for never read
Strangers like you that pictured countenance,
The depth and passion of its earnest glance,
But to myself they turned (since none puts by
The curtain I have drawn for you, but I)
And seemed as they would ask me, if they durst,
How such a glance came there; so, not the first
Are you to turn and ask thus. Sir, 'twas not
Her husband's presence only, called that spot
Of joy into the Duchess' cheek: perhaps
Frà Pandolf chanced to say 'Her mantle laps
Over my Lady's wrist too much,' or 'Paint
Must never hope to reproduce the faint
Half-flush that dies along her throat:' such stuff
Was courtesy, she thought, and cause enough

For calling up that spot of joy. She had
A heart . . . how shall I say? . . . too soon made glad,
Too easily impressed; she liked whate'er
She looked on, and her looks went everywhere.
Sir, 'twas all one! My favour at her breast,
The dropping of the daylight in the West,
The bough of cherries some officious fool
Broke in the orchard for her, the white mule
She rode with round the terrace — all and each
Would draw from her alike the approving speech,
Or blush, at least. She thanked men, — good! but thanked
Somehow . . . I know not how . . . as if she ranked
My gift of a nine-hundred-years-old name
With anybody's gift. Who'd stoop to blame
This sort of trifling? Even had you skill
In speech — (which I have not) — to make your will
Quite clear to such an one, and say 'Just this
Or that in you disgusts me; here you miss,
Or there exceed the mark' — and if she let
Herself be lessoned so, nor plainly set
Her wits to yours, forsooth, and made excuse,
— E'en then would be some stooping; and I choose
Never to stoop. Oh Sir, she smiled, no doubt,
Whene'er I passed her; but who passed without

Much the same smile? This grew; I gave commands;
Then all smiles stopped together. There she stands
As if alive. Will't please you rise? We'll meet
The company below, then. I repeat,
The Count your Master's known munificence
Is ample warrant that no just pretence
Of mine for dowry will be disallowed;
Though his fair daughter's self, as I avowed
At starting, is my object. Nay, we'll go
Together down, Sir. Notice Neptune, though,
Taming a sea-horse, thought a rarity,
Which Claus of Innsbruck cast in bronze for me!

The Pied Piper Of Hamelin

A Child's Story

(Written for, and inscribed to W. M. the Younger)

I

Hamelin Town's in Brunswick,
By famous Hanover city;
The river Weser, deep and wide,
Washes its wall on the southern side;
A pleasanter spot you never spied;
But, when begins my ditty,
Almost five hundred years ago,
To see the townsfolk suffer so
From vermin, was a pity.

II

Rats!
They fought the dogs and killed the cats,
And bit the babies in the cradles,
And ate the cheeses out of the vats,
And licked the soup from the cooks' own ladles,
Split open the kegs of salted sprats,
Made nests inside men's Sunday hats,

And even spoiled the women's chats,
By drowning their speaking
With shrieking and squeaking
In fifty different sharps and flats.

III

At last the people in a body
To the Town Hall came flocking:
'Tis clear,' cried they, 'our Mayor's a noddy;
And as for our Corporation — shocking
To think we buy gowns lined with ermine
For dolts that can't or won't determine
What's best to rid us of our vermin!
You hope, because you're old and obese,
To find in the furry civic robe ease?
Rouse up, Sirs! Give your brains a racking
To find a remedy we're lacking,
Or, sure as fate, we'll send you packing!'
At this the Mayor and Corporation
Quaked with a mighty consternation.

IV

An hour they sat in council,
At length the Mayor broke silence:

'For a guilder I'd my ermine gown sell,
I wish I were a mile hence!
It's easy to bid one rack one's brain —
I'm sure my poor head aches again
I've scratched it so, and all in vain.
Oh for a trap, a trap, a trap!'
Just as he said this, what should hap
At the chamber door but a gentle tap?
'Bless us,' cried the Mayor, 'what's that?'
(With the Corporation as he sat,
Looking little though wondrous fat;
Nor brighter was his eye, nor moister
Than a too-long-opened oyster,
Save when at noon his paunch grew mutinous
For a plate of turtle green and glutinous)
'Only a scraping of shoes on the mat?
Anything like the sound of a rat
Makes my heart go pit-a-pat!'

V

'Come in!' — the Mayor cried, looking bigger.
And in did come the strangest figure!
His queer long coat from heel to head
Was half of yellow and half of red,

23

And he himself was tall and thin,
With sharp blue eyes, each like a pin,
And light loose hair, yet swarthy skin,
No tuft on cheek nor beard on chin,
But lips where smiles went out and in;
There was no guessing his kith and kin:
And nobody could enough admire
The tall man and his quaint attire.
Quoth one: 'It's as my great-grandsire,
Starting up at the Trump of Doom's tone,
Had walked this way from his painted tombstone!'

VI

He advanced to the council-table:
And, 'Please your honours,' said he, 'I'm able,
By means of a secret charm to draw
All creatures living beneath the sun,
That creep or swim or fly or run,
After me so as you never saw!
And I chiefly use my charm
On creatures that do people harm,
The mole and toad and newt and viper;
And people call me the Pied Piper.'
(And here they noticed round his neck

A scarf of red and yellow stripe,
To match with his coat of the self-same cheque;
And at the scarf's end hung a pipe;
And his fingers, they noticed, were ever straying
As if impatient to be playing
Upon this pipe, as low it dangled
Over his vesture so old-fangled.)
'Yet,' said he, 'poor piper as I am,
In Tartary I freed the Cham,
Last June, from his huge swarms of gnats;
I eased in Asia the Nizam
Of a monstrous brood of vampyre-bats:
And as for what your brain bewilders,
If I can rid your town of rats
Will you give a thousand guilders?'
'One? fifty thousand!' — was the exclamation
Of the astonished Mayor and Corporation.

VII

Into the street the Piper stept,
Smiling first a little smile,
As if he knew what magic slept
In his quiet pipe the while;
Then, like a musical adept,

25

To blow the pipe his lips he wrinkled,
And green and blue his sharp eyes twinkled
Like a candle-flame where salt is sprinkled;
And ere three shrill notes the pipe uttered,
You heard as if an army muttered;
And the muttering grew to a grumbling;
And the grumbling grew to a mighty rumbling;
And out of the houses the rats came tumbling.
Great rats, small rats, lean rats, brawny rats,
Brown rats, black rats, grey rats, tawny rats,
Grave old plodders, gay young friskers,
Fathers, mothers, uncles, cousins,
Cocking tails and pricking whiskers,
Families by tens and dozens,
Brothers, sisters, husbands, wives —
Followed the Piper for their lives.
From street to street he piped advancing,
And step for step they followed dancing,
Until they came to the river Weser
Wherein all plunged and perished!
— Save one who, stout as Julius Caesar,
Swam across and lived to carry
(As he, the manuscript he cherished)
To Rat-land home his commentary:

Which was, 'At the first shrill notes of the pipe,
I heard a sound as of scraping tripe,
And putting apples, wondrous ripe,
Into a cider-press's gripe:
And a moving away of pickle-tub-boards,
And a leaving ajar of conserve-cupboards,
And a drawing the corks of train-oil-flasks,
And a breaking the hoops of butter-casks:
And it seemed as if a voice
(Sweeter far than bý harp or bý psaltery
Is breathed) called out, "Oh rats, rejoice!
The world is grown to one vast drysaltery!
So munch on, crunch on, take your nuncheon,
Breakfast, supper, dinner, luncheon!"
And just as a bulky sugar-puncheon,
All ready staved, like a great sun shone
Glorious scarce an inch before me,
Just as methought it said, "Come, bore me!"
— I found the Weser rolling o'er me.'

VIII

You should have heard the Hamelin people
Ringing the bells till they rocked the steeple.
'Go,' cried the Mayor, 'and get long poles!

Poke out the nests and block up the holes!
Consult with carpenters and builders,
And leave in our town not even a trace
Of the rats!' — when suddenly, up the face
Of the Piper perked in the market-place,
With a, 'First, if you please, my thousand guilders!'

IX

A thousand guilders! The Mayor looked blue;
So did the Corporation too.
For council dinners made rare havoc
With Claret, Moselle, Vin-de-Grave, Hock;
And half the money would replenish
Their cellar's biggest butt with Rhenish.
To pay this sum to a wandering fellow
With a gipsy coat of red and yellow!
'Beside,' quoth the Mayor with a knowing wink,
'Our business was done at the river's brink;
We saw with our eyes the vermin sink,
And what's dead can't come to life, I think.
So, friend, we're not the folks to shrink
From the duty of giving you something for drink,
And a matter of money to put in your poke;
But as for the guilders, what we spoke

Of them, as you very well know, was in joke.
Beside, our losses have made us thrifty.
A thousand guilders! Come, take fifty!'

X

The piper's face fell, and he cried,
'No trifling! I can't wait, beside!
I've promised to visit by dinner time
Bagdat, and accept the prime
Of the Head-Cook's potage, all he's rich in,
For having left, in the Caliph's kitchen,
Of a nest of scorpions no survivor —
With him I proved no bargain-driver,
With you, don't think I'll bate a stiver!
And folks who put me in a passion
May find me pipe to another fashion.'

XI

'How?' cried the Mayor, 'd'ye think I brook
Being worse treated than a Cook?
Insulted by a lazy ribald
With idle pipe and vesture piebald?
You threaten us, fellow? Do your worst,
Blow your pipe there till you burst!'

Once more he stept into the street
And to his lips again
Laid his long pipe of smooth straight cane;
And ere he blew three notes (such sweet
Soft notes as yet musician's cunning
Never gave the enraptured air)
There was a rustling, that seemed like a bustling
Of merry crowds justling at pitching and hustling,
Small feet were pattering, wooden shoes clattering,
Little hands clapping and little tongues chattering,
And, like fowls in a farm-yard when barley is scattering,
Out come the children running.
All the little boys and girls,
With rosy cheeks and flaxen curls,
And sparkling eyes and teeth like pearls,
Tripping and skipping, ran merrily after
The wonderful music with shouting and laughter.

The Mayor was dumb, and the Council stood
As if they were changed into blocks of wood,
Unable to move a step, or cry

To the children merrily skipping by
— Could only follow with the eye
That joyous crowd at the Piper's back.
But how the Mayor was on the rack,
And the wretched Council's bosoms beat,
As the Piper turned from the High Street
To where the Weser rolled its waters
Right in the way of their sons and daughters!
However he turned from South to West,
And to Koppelberg Hill his steps addressed,
And after him the children pressed;
Great was the joy in every breast.
'He never can cross that mighty top!
He's forced to let the piping drop,
And we shall see our children stop!'
When, lo, as they reached the mountainside,
A wondrous portal opened wide,
As if a cavern was suddenly hollowed;
And the Piper advanced and the children followed,
And when all were in to the very last,
The door in the mountainside shut fast.
Did I say, all? No! One was lame,
And could not dance the whole of the way;
And in after years, if you would blame

His sadness, he was used to say, —
'It's dull in our town since my playmates left!
I can't forget that I'm bereft
Of all the pleasant sights they see,
Which the Piper also promised me.
For he led us, he said, to a joyous land,
Joining the town and just at hand,
Where waters gushed and fruit-trees grew,
And flowers put forth a fairer hue,
And everything was strange and new;
The sparrows were brighter than peacocks here,
And their dogs outran our fallow deer,
And honey-bees had lost their stings,
And horses were born with eagles' wings:
And just as I became assured
My lame foot would be speedily cured,
The music stopped and I stood still,
And found myself outside the Hill,
Left alone against my will,
To go now limping as before,
And never hear of that country more!'

Alas, alas for Hamelin!
There came into many a burgher's pate
A text which says that Heaven's Gate
Opes to the Rich at as easy rate
As the needle's eye takes a camel in!
The Mayor sent East, West, North and South,
To offer the Piper, by word of mouth,
Wherever it was men's lot to find him,
Silver and gold to his heart's content,
If he'd only return the way he went,
And bring the children behind him.
But when they saw 'twas a lost endeavour,
And Piper and dancers were gone for ever,
They made a decree that lawyers never
Should think their records dated duly
If, after the day of the month and year,
These words did not as well appear,
'And so long after what happened here
On the Twenty-second of July,
Thirteen hundred and seventy-six:'
And the better in memory to fix
The place of the children's last retreat,
They called it, the Pied Piper's Street —

Where any one playing on pipe or tabor
Was sure for the future to lose his labour.
Nor suffered they hostelry or tavern
To shock with mirth a street so solemn;
But opposite the place of the cavern
They wrote the story on a column,
And on the great church-window painted
The same, to make the world acquainted
How their children were stolen away,
And there it stands to this very day.
And I must not omit to say
That in Transylvania there's a tribe
Of alien people who ascribe
The outlandish ways and dress
On which their neighbours lay such stress,
To their fathers and mothers having risen
Out of some subterraneous prison
Into which they were trepanned
Long time ago in a mighty band
Out of Hamelin town in Brunswick land,
But how or why, they don't understand.

XV

So, Willy, let me and you be wipers
Of scores out with all men — especially pipers!
And, whether they pipe us free, from rats or from mice,
If we've promised them aught, let us keep our promise!

PORPHYRIA'S LOVER

The rain set early in to-night,
The sullen wind was soon awake,
It tore the elm-tops down for spite,
And did its worst to vex the lake:
I listened with heart fit to break.
When glided in Porphyria; straight
She shut the cold out and the storm,
And kneeled and made the cheerless grate
Blaze up, and all the cottage warm;
Which done, she rose, and from her form
Withdrew the dripping cloak and shawl,
And laid her soiled gloves by, untied
Her hat and let the damp hair fall,
And, last, she sat down by my side
And called me. When no voice replied,
She put my arm about her waist,
And made her smooth white shoulder bare,
And all her yellow hair displaced,
And, stooping, made my cheek lie there,
And spread o'er all her yellow hair,
Murmuring how she loved me — she
Too weak, for all her heart's endeavour,

To set its struggling passion free
From pride, and vainer ties dissever,
And give herself to me for ever.
But passion sometimes would prevail,
Nor could to-night's gay feast restrain
A sudden thought of one so pale
For love of her, and all in vain:
So, she was come through wind and rain.
Be sure I looked up at her eyes
Happy and proud; at last I knew
Porphyria worshipped me; surprise
Made my heart swell, and still it grew
While I debated what to do.
That moment she was mine, mine, fair,
Perfectly pure and good: I found
A thing to do, and all her hair
In one long yellow string I wound
Three times her little throat around,
And strangled her. No pain felt she;
I am quite sure she felt no pain.
As a shut bud that holds a bee,
I warily oped her lids: again
Laughed the blue eyes without a stain.
And I untightened next the tress

About her neck; her cheek once more
Blushed bright beneath my burning kiss:
I propped her head up as before,
Only, this time my shoulder bore
Her head, which droops upon it still:
The smiling rosy little head,
So glad it has its utmost will,
That all it scorned at once is fled,
And I, its love, am gained instead!
Porphyria's love: she guessed not how
Her darling one wish would be heard.
And thus we sit together now,
And all night long we have not stirred,
And yet God has not said a word!

CHRISTMAS EVE

I

Out of the little chapel I burst
Into the fresh night-air again.
Five minutes full, I waited first
In the doorway, to escape the rain
That drove in gusts down the common's centre
At the edge of which the chapel stands,
Before I plucked up heart to enter.
Heaven knows how many sorts of hands
Reached past me, groping for the latch
Of the inner door that hung on catch
More obstinate the more they fumbled,
Till, giving way at last with a scold
Of the crazy hinge, in squeezed or tumbled
One sheep more to the rest in fold,
And left me irresolute, standing sentry
In the sheepfold's lath-and-plaster entry,
Six feet long by three feet wide,
Partitioned off from the vast inside —
I blocked up half of it at least.
No remedy; the rain kept driving.
They eyed me much as some wild beast,
That congregation, still arriving,

Some of them by the main road, white
A long way past me into the night,
Skirting the common, then diverging;
Not a few suddenly emerging
From the common's self thro' the paling-gaps,
— They house in the gravel-pits perhaps,
Where the road stops short with its safeguard border
Of lamps, as tired of such disorder; —
But the most turned in yet more abruptly
  From a certain squalid knot of alleys,
Where the town's bad blood once slept corruptly,
  Which now the little chapel rallies
And leads into day again, — its priestliness
Lending itself to hide their beastliness
So cleverly (thanks in part to the mason),
And putting so cheery a whitewashed face on
Those neophytes too much in lack of it,
  That, where you cross the common as I did,
  And meet the party thus presided,
'Mount Zion' with Love-lane at the back of it,
They front you as little disconcerted
As, bound for the hills, her fate averted,
And her wicked people made to mind him,
Lot might have marched with Gomorrah behind him.

II

Well, from the road, the lanes or the common,
In came the flock: the fat weary woman,
Panting and bewildered, down-clapping
    Her umbrella with a mighty report,
Grounded it by me, wry and flapping,
    A wreck of whalebones; then, with a snort,
Like a startled horse, at the interloper
(Who humbly knew himself improper,
But could not shrink up small enough)
— Round to the door, and in, — the gruff
Hinge's invariable scold
Making my very blood run cold.
Prompt in the wake of her, up-pattered
On broken clogs, the many-tattered
Little old-faced peaking sister-turned-mother
Of the sickly babe she tried to smother
Somehow up, with its spotted face,
From the cold, on her breast, the one warm place;
She too must stop, wring the poor ends dry
Of a draggled shawl, and add thereby
Her tribute to the door-mat, sopping
Already from my own clothes' dropping,
Which yet she seemed to grudge I should stand on:

Then, stooping down to take off her pattens,
She bore them defiantly, in each hand one,
Planted together before her breast
And its babe, as good as a lance in rest.
    Close on her heels, the dingy satins
Of a female something, past me flitted,
    With lips as much too white, as a streak
    Lay far too red on each hollow cheek;
And it seemed the very door-hinge pitied
All that was left of a woman once,
Holding at least its tongue for the nonce.
Then a tall yellow man, like the Penitent Thief,
With his jaw bound up in a handkerchief,
And eyelids screwed together tight,
Led himself in by some inner light.
And, except from him, from each that entered,
    I got the same interrogation —
'What, you the alien, you have ventured
    To take with us, the elect, your station?
A carer for none of it, a Gallio!' —
    Thus, plain as print, I read the glance
At a common prey, in each countenance
    As of huntsman giving his hounds the tallyho.
And, when the door's cry drowned their wonder,

The draught, it always sent in shutting,
Made the flame of the single tallow candle
In the cracked square lantern I stood under,
  Shoot its blue lip at me, rebutting
As it were, the luckless cause of scandal:
I verily fancied the zealous light
(In the chapel's secret, too!) for spite
Would shudder itself clean off the wick,
With the airs of a Saint John's Candlestick.
There was no standing it much longer.
'Good folks,' thought I, as resolve grew stronger,
'This way you perform the Grand-Inquisitor
When the weather sends you a chance visitor?
You are the men, and wisdom shall die with you,
And none of the old Seven Churches vie with you!
But still, despite the pretty perfection
  To which you carry your trick of exclusiveness,
And, taking God's word under wise protection,
  Correct its tendency to diffusiveness,
And bid one reach it over hot ploughshares, —
  Still, as I say, though you've found salvation,
If I should choose to cry, as now, "Shares!" —
  See if the best of you bars me my ration!
I prefer, if you please, for my expounder

43

Of the laws of the feast, the feast's own Founder;
Mine's the same right with you poorest and sickliest
    Supposing I don the marriage vestiment:
    So, shut your mouth and open your Testament,
And carve me my portion at your quickliest!'
Accordingly, as a shoemaker's lad
    With wizened face in want of soap,
    And wet apron wound round his waist like a rope,
(After stopping outside, for his cough was bad,
To get the fit over, poor gentle creature,
And so avoid disturbing the preacher)
— Passed in, I sent my elbow spikewise
At the shutting door, and entered likewise,
Received the hinge's accustomed greeting,
    And crossed the threshold's magic pentacle,
    And found myself in full conventicle,
— To wit, in Zion Chapel Meeting,
On the Christmas-Eve of 'Forty-nine,
    Which, calling its flock to their special clover,
    Found all assembled and one sheep over,
Whose lot, as the weather pleased, was mine.

III

I very soon had enough of it.
    The hot smell and the human noises,
And my neighbour's coat, the greasy cuff of it,
    Were a pebble-stone that a child's hand poises,
Compared with the pig-of-lead-like pressure
    Of the preaching man's immense stupidity,
As he poured his doctrine forth, full measure,
    To meet his audience's avidity.
You needed not the wit of the Sibyl
    To guess the cause of it all, in a twinkling:
    No sooner our friend had got an inkling
Of treasure hid in the Holy Bible,
(Whene'er 'twas the thought first struck him,
How death, at unawares, might duck him
Deeper than the grave, and quench
The gin-shop's light in hell's grim drench)
Than he handled it so, in fine irreverence,
    As to hug the book of books to pieces:
And, a patchwork of chapters and texts in severance,
    Not improved by the private dog's—ears and creases,
Having clothed his own soul with, he'd fain see equipt

yours, —

So tossed you again your Holy Scriptures.

And you picked them up, in a sense, no doubt:
Nay, had but a single face of my neighbours
Appeared to suspect that the preacher's labours
Were help which the world could be saved without,
'Tis odds but I might have borne in quiet
A qualm or two at my spiritual diet,
Or (who can tell?) perchance even mustered
Somewhat to urge in behalf of the sermon:
But the flock sat on, divinely flustered.
Sniffing, methought, its dew of Hermon
With such content in every snuffle,
As the devil inside us loves to ruffle.
My old fat woman purred with pleasure,
And thumb round thumb went twirling faster,
While she, to his periods keeping measure,
Maternally devoured the pastor.
The man with the handkerchief untied it,
Showed us a horrible wen inside it,
Gave his eyelids yet another screwing,
And rocked himself as the woman was doing.
The shoemaker's lad, discreetly choking,
Kept down his cough. 'Twas too provoking!
My gorge rose at the nonsense and stuff of it;
So, saying like Eve when she plucked the apple,

'I wanted a taste, and now there's enough of it,'
I flung out of the little chapel.

IV

There was a lull in the rain, a lull
    In the wind too; the moon was risen,
And would have shone out pure and full,
    But for the ramparted cloud-prison,
Block on block built up in the West,
For what purpose the wind knows best,
Who changes his mind continually.
And the empty other half of the sky
Seemed in its silence as if it knew
What, any moment, might look through
A chance gap in that fortress massy: —
    Through its fissures you got hints
    Of the flying moon, by the shifting tints,
Now, a dull lion-colour, now, brassy
Burning to yellow, and whitest yellow,
Like furnace-smoke just ere flames bellow,
All a-simmer with intense strain
To let her through, — then blank again,
At the hope of her appearance failing.
Just by the chapel, a break in the railing

Shows a narrow path directly across;
'Tis ever dry walking there, on the moss —
Besides, you go gently all the way uphill.
    I stooped under and soon felt better;
My head grew lighter, my limbs more supple,
    As I walked on, glad to have slipt the fetter.
My mind was full of the scene I had left,
    That placid flock, that pastor vociferant,
    — How this outside was pure and different!
The sermon, now — what a mingled weft
Of good and ill! Were either less,
    Its fellow had coloured the whole distinctly;
But alas for the excellent earnestness,
    And the truths, quite true if stated succinctly,
But as surely false, in their quaint presentment,
However to pastor and flock's contentment!
Say rather, such truths looked false to your eyes,
    With his provings and parallels twisted and twined,
Till how could you know them, grown double their size
    In the natural fog of the good man's mind,
Like yonder spots of our roadside lamps,
Haloed about with the common's damps?
Truth remains true, the fault's in the prover;
    The zeal was good, and the aspiration;

And yet, and yet, fifty times over,
   Pharaoh received no demonstration,
By his Baker's dreams of Baskets Three,
Of the doctrine of the Trinity, —
Although, as our preacher thus embellished it,
Apparently his hearers relished it
With so unfeigned a gust — who knows if
They did not prefer our friend to Joseph?
But so it is everywhere, one way with all of them!
   These people have really felt, no doubt,
A something, the motion they style the Call of them;
   And this is their method of bringing about,
By a mechanism of words and tones,
(So many texts in so many groans)
A sort of reviving and reproducing,
   More or less perfectly, (who can tell?)
The mood itself, which strengthens by using;
   And how that happens, I understand well.
A tune was born in my head last week,
Out of the thump-thump and shriek-shriek
   Of the train, as I came by it, up from Manchester;
And when, next week, I take it back again,
My head will sing to the engine's clack again,
   While it only makes my neighbour's haunches stir,

49

— Finding no dormant musical sprout
In him, as in me, to be jolted out.
'Tis the taught already that profits by teaching;
He gets no more from the railway's preaching
    Than, from this preacher who does the rail's office, I:
Whom therefore the flock cast a jealous eye on.
Still, why paint over their door 'Mount Zion',
    To which all flesh shall come, saith the prophecy?

V

But wherefore be harsh on a single case?
    After how many modes, this Christmas-Eve,
Does the self-same weary thing take place?
    The same endeavour to make you believe,
And with much the same effect, no more:
    Each method abundantly convincing,
As I say, to those convinced before,
    But scarce to be swallowed without wincing
By the not-as-yet-convinced. For me,
I have my own church equally:
And in this church my faith sprang first!
    (I said, as I reached the rising ground,
And the wind began again, with a burst
    Of rain in my face, and a glad rebound

50

From the heart beneath, as if, God speeding me,
I entered his church-door, nature leading me)
— In youth I looked to these very skies,
And probing their immensities,
I found God there, his visible power;
     Yet felt in my heart, amid all its sense
     Of the power, an equal evidence
That his love, there too, was the nobler dower.
For the loving worm within its clod,
Were diviner than a loveless god
Amid his worlds, I will dare to say.
     You know what I mean: God's all, man's nought:
     But also, God, whose pleasure brought
Man into being, stands away
     As it were a handbreadth off, to give
Room for the newly-made to live,
And look at him from a place apart,
And use his gifts of brain and heart,
Given, indeed, but to keep for ever.
Who speaks of man, then, must not sever
Man's very elements from man,
Saying, 'But all is God's' — whose plan
Was to create man and then leave him
Able, his own word saith, to grieve him,

But able to glorify him too,
As a mere machine could never do,
That prayed or praised, all unaware
Of its fitness for aught but praise and prayer,
Made perfect as a thing of course.
Man, therefore, stands on his own stock
Of love and power as a pin-point rock:
And, looking to God who ordained divorce
Of the rock from his boundless continent,
Sees, in his power made evident,
Only excess by a million-fold
O'er power God gave man in the mould.
For, note: man's hand, first formed to carry
A few pounds' weight, when taught to marry
Its strength with an engine's, lifts a mountain,
    — Advancing in power by one degree;
    And why count steps through eternity?
But love is the ever-springing fountain:
Man may enlarge or narrow his bed
For the water's play, but the water-head —
How can he multiply or reduce it?
    As easy create it, as cause it to cease;
He may profit by it, or abuse it,
    But 'tis not a thing to bear increase

As power does: be love less or more
In the heart of man, he keeps it shut
Or opes it wide, as he pleases, but
Love's sum remains what it was before.
So, gazing up, in my youth, at love
As seen through power, ever above
All modes which make it manifest,
My soul brought all to a single test —
That he, the Eternal First and Last,
Who, in his power, had so surpassed
All man conceives of what is might, —
Whose wisdom, too, showed infinite,
— Would prove as infinitely good;
Would never, (my soul understood,)
With power to work all love desires,
Bestow e'en less than man requires;
That he who endlessly was teaching,
Above my spirit's utmost reaching,
What love can do in the leaf or stone,
(So that to master this alone,
This done in the stone or leaf for me,
I must go on learning endlessly)
Would never need that I, in turn,
Should point him out defect unheeded,

And show that God had yet to learn
    What the meanest human creature needed,
— Not life, to wit, for a few short years,
Tracking his way through doubts and fears,
While the stupid earth on which I stay
    Suffers no change, but passive adds
    Its myriad years to myriads,
Though I, he gave it to, decay,
Seeing death come and choose about me,
And my dearest ones depart without me.
No: love which, on earth, amid all the shows of it,
    Has ever been seen the sole good of life in it,
The love, ever growing there, spite of the strife in it,
    Shall arise, made perfect, from death's repose of it.
And I shall behold thee, face to face,
O God, and in thy light retrace
How in all I loved here, still wast thou!
Whom pressing to, then, as I fain would now,
I shall find as able to satiate
    The love, thy gift, as my spirit's wonder
Thou art able to quicken and sublimate,
    With this sky of thine, that I now walk under,
And glory in thee for, as I gaze
Thus, thus! Oh, let men keep their ways

Of seeking thee in a narrow shrine —
Be this my way! And this is mine!

VI

For lo, what think you? suddenly
The rain and the wind ceased, and the sky
Received at once the full fruition
Of the moon's consummate apparition.
The black cloud-barricade was riven,
Ruined beneath her feet, and driven
Deep in the West; while, bare and breathless,
   North and South and East lay ready
For a glorious thing that, dauntless, deathless,
   Sprang across them and stood steady.
'Twas a moon-rainbow, vast and perfect
From heaven to heaven extending, perfect
As the mother-moon's self, full in face.
It rose, distinctly at the base
   With its seven proper colours chorded,
Which still, in the rising, were compressed,
Until at last they coalesced,
   And supreme the spectral creature lorded
In a triumph of whitest white, —
   Above which intervened the night.

But above night too, like only the next,
  The second of a wondrous sequence,
  Reaching in rare and rarer frequence,
Till the heaven of heavens were circumflexed,
Another rainbow rose, a mightier,
Fainter, flushier and flightier, —
Rapture dying along its verge.
Oh, whose foot shall I see emerge,
Whose, from the straining topmost dark,
On to the keystone of that arc?

VII

This sight was shown me, there and then, —
Me, one out of a world of men,
Singled forth, as the chance might hap
To another if, in a thunderclap
Where I heard noise and you saw flame,
Some one man knew God called his name.
For me, I think I said, 'Appear!
Good were it to be ever here.
If thou wilt, let me build to thee
Service-tabernacles three,
Where, forever in thy presence,
In ecstatic acquiescence,

Far alike from thriftless learning
And ignorance's undiscerning,
I may worship and remain!'
   Thus at the show above me, gazing
With upturned eyes, I felt my brain
   Glutted with the glory, blazing
Throughout its whole mass, over and under
Until at length it burst asunder
And out of it bodily there streamed,
The too-much glory, as it seemed,
Passing from out me to the ground,
Then palely serpentining round
Into the dark with mazy error.

VIII

All at once I looked up with terror.
He was there.
He Himself with His human air.
On the narrow pathway, just before.
I saw the back of Him, no more —
He had left the chapel, then, as I.
I forgot all about the sky.
No face: only the sight
Of a sweepy garment, vast and white,

With a hem that I could recognize.
I felt terror, no surprise;
My mind filled with the cataract,
At one bound of the mighty fact.
I remember, He did say
    Doubtless that, to this world's end,
Where two or three should meet and pray,
    He would be in the midst, their friend;
Certainly He was there with them!
    And my pulses leaped for joy
    Of the golden thought without alloy,
That I saw His very vesture's hem.
Then rushed the blood back, cold and clear,
With a fresh enhancing shiver of fear;
And I hastened, cried out while I pressed
To the salvation of the Vest,
But not so, Lord! It cannot be
That Thou, indeed, art leaving me —
Me, that have despised Thy friends!
Did my heart make no amends?
Thou art the love of God — above
His power, didst hear me place His love,
And that was leaving the world for Thee.
Therefore Thou must not turn from me

As I had chosen the other part!
Folly and pride o'ercame my heart.
Our best is bad, nor bears Thy test;
Still, it should be our very best.
I thought it best that Thou, the Spirit,
    Be worshipped in spirit and in truth,
And in beauty, as even we require it —
    Not in the forms burlesque, uncouth,
I left but now, as scarcely fitted
For Thee: I knew not what I pitied.
But, all I felt there, right or wrong,
    What is it to Thee, who curest sinning?
Am I not weak as Thou art strong?
    I have looked to Thee from the beginning,
Straight up to Thee through all the world
Which, like an idle scroll, lay furled
To nothingness on either side:
And since the time Thou wast descried,
Spite of the weak heart, so have I
Lived ever, and so fain would die,
Living and dying, Thee before!
But if Thou leavest me —

IX

Less or more,
I suppose that I spoke thus.
When, — have mercy, Lord, on us!
The whole face turned upon me full.
*   And I spread myself beneath it,*
*   As when the bleacher spreads, to seethe it*
In the cleansing sun, his wool, —
*   Steeps in the flood of noontide whiteness*
*   Some defiled, discoloured web —*
So lay I, saturate with brightness.
*   And when the flood appeared to ebb,*
Lo, I was walking, light and swift,
*   With my senses settling fast and steadying,*
But my body caught up in the whirl and drift
*   Of the Vesture's amplitude, still eddying*
On, just before me, still to be followed,
*   As it carried me after with its motion:*
What shall I say? — as a path were hollowed
*   And a man went weltering through the ocean,*
Sucked along in the flying wake
Of the luminous water-snake.
Darkness and cold were cloven, as through
I passed, upborne yet walking too.

And I turned to myself at intervals, —
'So He said, so it befalls.
God who registers the cup
    Of mere cold water, for His sake
To a disciple rendered up,
    Disdains not His own thirst to slake
At the poorest love was ever offered:
And because my heart I proffered,
With true love trembling at the brim,
He suffers me to follow Him
For ever, my own way, — dispensed
From seeking to be influenced
By all the less immediate ways
    That earth, in worships manifold,
Adopts to reach, by prayer and praise,
    The garment's hem, which, lo, I hold!'

                    X
And so we crossed the world and stopped.
    For where am I, in city or plain,
    Since I am 'ware of the world again?
And what is this that rises propped
With pillars of prodigious girth?
    Is it really on the earth,

This miraculous Dome of God?
Has the angel's measuring-rod
Which numbered cubits, gem from gem,
'Twixt the gates of the New Jerusalem,
Meted it out, — and what he meted,
Have the sons of men completed?
— Binding, ever as He bade,
Columns in the colonnade
With arms wide open to embrace
The entry of the human race
To the breast of . . . what is it, yon building,
Ablaze in front, all paint and gilding,
With marble for brick, and stone of price
For garniture of the edifice?
Now I see; it is no dream;
It stands there and it does not seem:
For ever, in pictures, thus it looks,
And thus I have read of it in books
Often in England, leagues away,
And wondered how these fountains play,
Growing up eternally
Each to a musical water-tree,
Whose blossoms drop, a glittering boon,
Before my eyes, in the light of the moon,

To the granite lavers underneath.
Liar and dreamer in your teeth!
I, the sinner that speak to you,
Was in Rome this night, and stood, and knew
Both this and more. For see, for see,
The dark is rent, mine eye is free
To pierce the crust of the outer wall,
And I view inside, and all there, all,
As the swarming hollow of a hive,
The whole Basilica alive!
Men in the chancel, body and nave,
Men on the pillars' architrave,
Men on the statues, men on the tombs
With popes and kings in their porphyry wombs,
All famishing in expectation
Of the main-altar's consummation.
For see, for see, the rapturous moment
Approaches, and earth's best endowment
Blends with heaven's; the taper-fires
Pant up, the winding brazen spires
Heave loftier yet the baldachin;
The incense-gaspings, long kept in,
Suspire in clouds; the organ blatant
Holds his breath and grovels latent,

As if God's hushing finger grazed him,
(Like Behemoth when He praised him)
At the silver bell's shrill tinkling,
Quick cold drops of terror sprinkling
On the sudden pavement strewed
With faces of the multitude.
Earth breaks up, time drops away,
In flows heaven, with its new day
Of endless life, when He who trod,
Very man and very God,
This earth in weakness, shame and pain,
Dying the death whose signs remain
Up yonder on the accursed tree, —
Shall come again, no more to be
Of captivity the thrall,
But the one God, All in all,
King of kings, Lord of lords,
As His servant John received the words,
'I died, and live for evermore!'

XI

Yet I was left outside the door.
Why sit I here on the threshold-stone
Left till He return, alone
Save for the garment's extreme fold

Abandoned still to bless my hold?
My reason, to my doubt, replied,
As if a book were opened wide,
And at a certain page I traced
Every record undefaced,
Added by successive years, —
The harvestings of truth's stray ears
Singly gleaned, and in one sheaf
Bound together for belief.
Yes, I said — that He will go
And sit with these in turn, I know.
Their faith's heart beats, though her head swims
Too giddily to guide her limbs,
Disabled by their palsy-stroke
From propping mine. Though Rome's gross yoke
Drops off, no more to be endured,
Her teaching is not so obscured
By errors and perversities,
That no truth shines athwart the lies:
And He, whose eye detects a spark
Even where, to man's, the whole seems dark,
May well see flame where each beholder
Acknowledges the embers smoulder.
But I, a mere man, fear to quit
The clue God gave me as most fit

To guide my footsteps through life's maze,
Because Himself discerns all ways
Open to reach him: I, a man
Able to mark where faith began
To swerve aside, till from its summit
Judgement drops her damning plummet,
Pronouncing such a fatal space
Departed from the founder's base:
He will not bid me enter too,
But rather sit, as now I do,
Awaiting His return outside.
— 'Twas thus my reason straight replied
And joyously I turned, and pressed
The garment's skirt upon my breast,
Until, afresh its light suffusing me,
My heart cried — What has been abusing me
That I should wait here lonely and coldly,
Instead of rising, entering boldly,
Baring truth's face, and letting drift
Her veils of lies as they choose to shift?
Do these men praise Him? I will raise
My voice up to their point of praise!
I see the error; but above
The scope of error, see the love. —

Oh, love of those first Christian days!
— Fanned so soon into a blaze,
From the spark preserved by the trampled sect,
That the antique sovereign Intellect
Which then sat ruling in the world,
Like a change in dreams, was hurled
From the throne he reigned upon:
You looked up and he was gone.
Gone, his glory of the pen!
— Love, with Greece and Rome in ken,
Bade her scribes abhor the trick
Of poetry and rhetoric,
And exult with hearts set free,
In blessed imbecility
Scrawled, perchance, on some torn sheet
Leaving Sallust incomplete.
Gone, his pride of sculptor, painter!
— Love, while able to acquaint her
While the thousand statues yet
Fresh from chisel, pictures wet
From brush, she saw on every side,
Chose rather with an infant's pride
To frame those portents which impart
Such unction to true Christian Art.

Gone, music too! The air was stirred
By happy wings: Terpander's bird
(That, when the cold came, fled away)
Would tarry not the wintry day, —
As more-enduring sculpture must,
Till filthy saints rebuked the gust
With which they chanced to get a sight
Of some dear naked Aphrodite
They glanced a thought above the toes of,
By breaking zealously her nose off.
Love, surely, from that music's lingering,
Might have filched her organ-fingering,
Nor chosen rather to set prayings
To hog-grunts, praises to horse-neighings.
Love was the startling thing, the new:
Love was the all-sufficient too;
And seeing that, you see the rest:
As a babe can find its mother's breast
As well in darkness as in light,
Love shut our eyes, and all seemed right.
True, the world's eyes are open now:
— Less need for me to disallow
Some few that keep Love's zone unbuckled,
Peevish as ever to be suckled,

Lulled by the same old baby-prattle
With intermixture of the rattle,
When she would have them creep, stand steady
Upon their feet, or walk already,
Not to speak of trying to climb.
I will be wise another time,
And not desire a wall between us,
 When next I see a church-roof cover
So many species of one genus,
 All with foreheads bearing lover
Written above the earnest eyes of them;
 All with breasts that beat for beauty,
Whether sublimed, to the surprise of them,
 In noble daring, steadfast duty,
The heroic in passion, or in action, —
Or, lowered for sense's satisfaction,
To the mere outside of human creatures,
Mere perfect form and faultless features.
What? with all Rome here, whence to levy
 Such contributions to their appetite,
With women and men in a gorgeous bevy,
 They take, as it were, a padlock, clap it tight
On their southern eyes, restrained from feeding.
On the glories of their ancient reading,

On the beauties of their modern singing,
On the wonders of the builder's bringing,
On the majesties of Art around them, —
    And, all these loves, late struggling incessant,
When faith has at last united and bound them,
        They offer up to God for a present?
Why, I will, on the whole, be rather proud of it, —
    And, only taking the act in reference
To the other recipients who might have allowed it,
        I will rejoice that God had the preference.

XII

So I summed up my new resolves:
    Too much love there can never be,
And where the intellect devolves
    Its function on love exclusively,
I, a man who possesses both,
Will accept the provision, nothing loth,
— Will feast my love, then depart elsewhere,
That my intellect may find its share.
And ponder, O soul, the while thou departest,
And see thou applaud the great heart of the artist,
Who, examining the capabilities
    Of the block of marble he has to fashion

Into a type of thought or passion, —
Not always, using obvious facilities,
Shapes it, as any artist can,
Into a perfect symmetrical man,
Complete from head to foot of the life-size,
Such as old Adam stood in his wife's eyes, —
But, now and then, bravely aspires to consummate
A Colossus by no means so easy to come at,
And uses the whole of his block for the bust,
    Leaving the mind of the public to finish it,
Since cut it ruefully short he must:
On the face alone he expends his devotion,
    He rather would mar than resolve to diminish it,
    — Saying, 'Applaud me for this grand notion
Of what a face may be! As for completing it
    In breast and body and limbs, do that, you!'
All hail! I fancy how, happily meeting it,
    A trunk and legs would perfect the statue,
Could man carve so as to answer volition.
    And how much nobler than petty cavils,
    Were a hope to find, in my spirit-travels,
Some artist of another ambition,
Who having a block to carve, no bigger,
    Has spent his power on the opposite quest,

And believed to begin at the feet was best —
For so may I see, ere I die, the whole figure!

XIII

No sooner said than out in the night!
My heart beat lighter and more light:
And still, as before, I was walking swift,
*   With my senses settling fast and steadying,*
But my body caught up in the whirl and drift
*   Of the Vesture's amplitude, still eddying*
On just before me, still to be followed,
*   — What shall I say? — as a path were hollowed,*
*   And a man went weltering through the ocean,*
Sucked along in the flying wake
Of the luminous water-snake.

XIV

Alone! I am left along once more —
*   (Save for the garment's extreme fold*
*   Abandoned still to bless my hold)*
Alone, beside the entrance-door
Of a sort of temple, — perhaps a college,
— Like nothing I ever saw before

At home in England, to my knowledge.
The tall old quaint irregular town!
    It may be . . . though which, I can't affirm . . . any
    Of the famous middle-age towns of Germany;
And this flight of stairs where I sit down,
Is it Halle, Weimar, Cassel, Frankfort
Or Göttingen, I have to thank for't?
It may be Göttingen, — most likely.
Through the open door I catch obliquely
    Glimpses of a lecture-hall;
    And not a bad assembly neither,
Ranged decent and symmetrical
    On benches, waiting what's to see there;
Which, holding still by the Vesture's hem,
I also resolve to see with them,
Cautious this time how I suffer to slip
The chance of joining in fellowship
With any that call themselves His friends;
    As these folks do, I have a notion.
    But hist — a buzzing and emotion!
All settle themselves, the while ascends
By the creaking rail to the lecture-desk,
    Step by step, deliberate
    Because of his cranium's over-freight,

Three parts sublime to one grotesque,
If I have proved an accurate guesser,
The hawk-nosed high-cheek-boned Professor,
I felt at once as if there ran
A shoot of love from my heart to the man —
That sallow virgin-minded studious
    Martyr to mild enthusiasm,
As he uttered a kind of cough-preludious
    That woke my sympathetic spasm,
(Beside some spitting that made me sorry)
And stood, surveying his auditory
With a wan pure look, well nigh celestial, —
    Those blue eyes had survived so much!
    While, under the foot they could not smutch,
Lay all the fleshly and the bestial.
Over he bowed, and arranged his notes,
Till the auditory's clearing of throats
Was done with, died into a silence;
    And, when each glance was upward sent,
    Each bearded mouth composed intent,
And a pin might be heard drop half a mile hence, —
He pushed back higher his spectacles,
Let the eye stream out like lamps from cells,
And giving his head of hair — a hake

Of undressed tow, for colour and quantity —
One rapid and impatient shake,
*   (As our own Young England adjusts a jaunty tie*
When about to impart, on mature digestion,
Some thrilling view of the surplice-question)
— The Professor's grave voice, sweet though hoarse,
Broke into his Christmas-Eve discourse.

XV

And he began it by observing
*   How reason dictated that men*
Should rectify the natural swerving,
*   By a reversion, now and then,*
To the well-heads of knowledge, few
And far away, whence rolling grew
The life-stream wide whereat we drink,
Commingled, as we needs must think,
With waters alien to the source;
To do which, aimed this eve's discourse;
Since, where could be a fitter time
For tracing backward to its prime
This Christianity, this lake,
The reservoir, whereat we slake,
From on or other bank, our thirst?

So, he proposed inquiring first
Into the various sources whence
   This Myth of Christ is derivable;
Demanding from the evidence,
   (Since plainly no such life was liveable)
How these phenomena should class?
Whether 'twere best opine Christ was,
Or never was at all, or whether
He was and was not, both together —
It matters little for the name,
So the idea be left the same.
Only, for practical purpose' sake,
'Twas obviously as well to take
The popular story, — understanding
   How the ineptitude of the time,
And the penman's prejudice, expanding
   Fact into fable fit for the clime,
Had, by slow and sure degrees, translated it
   Into this myth, this Individuum, —
Which, when reason had strained and abated it
   Of foreign matter, left, for residuum,
A Man! — a right true man, however,
Whose work was worthy a man's endeavour:
Work, that gave warrant almost sufficient

To his disciples, for rather believing
He was just omnipotent and omniscient,
    As it gives to us, for as frankly receiving
His word, their tradition, — which, though it meant
Something entirely different
From all that those who only heard it,
In their simplicity thought and averred it,
Had yet a meaning quite as respectable:
For, among other doctrines delectable,
Was he not surely the first to insist on
    The natural sovereignty of our race? —
    Here the lecturer came to a pausing-place.
And while his cough, like a drouthy piston,
Tried to dislodge the husk that grew to him,
I seized the occasion of bidding adieu to him,
The Vesture still within my hand.

                    XVI

I could interpret its command.
This time He would not bid me enter
The exhausted air-bell of the Critic.
Truth's atmosphere may grow mephitic
When Papist struggles with Dissenter,
Impregnating its pristine clarity,

— One, by his daily fare's vulgarity,
Its gust of broken meat and garlic;
— One, by his soul's too-much presuming
To turn the frankincense's fuming
    And vapours of the candle starlike
Into the cloud her wings she buoys on.
    Each, that thus sets the pure air seething,
    May poison it for healthy breathing —
But the Critic leaves no air to poison;
Pumps out with ruthless ingenuity
Atom by atom, and leaves you — vacuity.
Thus much of Christ does he reject?
And what retain? His intellect?
What is it I must reverence duly?
Poor intellect for worship, truly,
Which tells me simply what was told
    (If mere morality, bereft
    Of the God in Christ, be all that's left)
Elsewhere by voices manifold;
With this advantage, that the stater
    Made nowise the important stumble
    Of adding, he, the sage and humble,
Was also one with the Creator.
You urge Christ's followers' simplicity:

But how does shifting blame, evade it?
Have wisdom's words no more felicity?
The stumbling-block, his speech — who laid it?
How comes it that for one found able
To sift the truth of it from fable,
Millions believe it to the letter?
Christ's goodness, then — does that fare better?
Strange goodness, which upon the score
Of being goodness, the mere due
Of man to fellow-man, much more
To God, — should take another view
Of its possessor's privilege,
And bid him rule his race! You pledge
Your fealty to such rule? what, all —
From heavenly John and Attic Paul,
And that brave weather-battered Peter,
Whose stout faith only stood completer
For buffets, sinning to be pardoned,
As, more his hands hauled nets, they hardened, —
All, down to you, the man of men,
Professing here at Göttingen,
Compose Christ's flock! They, you and I,
Are sheep of a good man! And why?
The goodness, — how did he acquire it?

Was it self-gained, did God inspire it?
Choose which; then tell me, on what ground
Should its possessor dare propound
His claim to rise o'er us an inch?
　　Were goodness all some man's invention,
　　Who arbitrarily made mention
What we should follow, and whence flinch, —
What qualities might take the style
　　Of right and wrong, — and had such guessing
　　Met with as general acquiescing
As graced the alphabet erewhile,
When A got leave an Ox to be,
No Camel (quoth the Jews) like G, —
For thus inventing thing and title
Worship were that man's fit requital.
But if the common conscience must
Be ultimately judge, adjust
Its apt name to each quality
Already known, — I would decree
Worship for such mere demonstration
　　And simple work of nomenclature,
　　Only the day I praised, not nature,
But Harvey, for the circulation.
I would praise such a Christ, with pride

And joy, that he, as none beside,
Had taught us how to keep the mind
God gave him, as God gave his kind,
Freer than they from fleshly taint:
I would call such a Christ our Saint,
As I declare our Poet, him
Whose insight makes all others dim:
A thousand poets pried at life,
And only one amid the strife
Rose to be Shakespeare: each shall take
His crown, I'd say, for the world's sake —
Though some objected — 'Had we seen
The heart and head of each, what screen
Was broken there to give them light,
While in ourselves it shuts the sight,
We should no more admire, perchance,
That these found truth out at a glance,
Than marvel how the bat discerns
Some pitch-dark cavern's fifty turns,
Led by a finer tact, a gift
He boasts, which other birds must shift
Without, and grope as best they can.'
No, freely I would praise the man, —
Nor one whit more, if he contended

That gift of his, from God descended.
Ah friend, what gift of man's does not?
No nearer something, by a jot,
Rise an infinity of nothings
 Than one: take Euclid for your teacher:
Distinguish kinds: do crownings, clothings,
 Make that creator which was creature?
Multiply gifts upon man's head,
And what, when all's done, shall be said
But — the more gifted he, I ween!
 That one's made Christ, this other, Pilate,
And this might be all that has been, —
 So what is there to frown or smile at?
What is left for us, save, in growth
Of soul, to rise up, far past both,
From the gift looking to the giver,
And from the cistern to the river,
And from the finite to infinity,
And from man's dust to God's divinity?

     XVII
Take all in a word: the truth in God's breast
Lies trace for trace upon ours impressed:
Though He is so bright and we so dim,

We are made in His image to witness Him:
And were no eye in us to tell,
    Instructed by no inner sense,
The light of heaven from the dark of hell,
    That light would want its evidence, —
Though justice, food and truth were still
Divine, if, by some demon's will,
Hatred and wrong had been proclaimed
Law through the worlds, and right misnamed.
No mere exposition of morality
Made or in part or in totality,
Should win you to give it worship, therefore:
And, if no better proof you will care for,
— Whom do you count the worst man upon earth?
    Be sure, he knows, in his conscience, more
Of what right is, than arrives at birth
    In the best man's acts that we bow before:
This last knows better — true, but my fact is,
'Tis one thing to know, and another to practise.
And thence I conclude that the real God-function
Is to furnish a motive and injunction
For practising what we know already.
And such an injunction and such a motive
As the God in Christ, do you waive, and 'heady,

High-minded,' hang your tablet-votive
Outside the fane on a finger-post?
Morality to the uttermost,
Supreme in Christ as we all confess,
Why need we prove would avail no jot
To make Him God, if God He were not?
What is the point where Himself lays stress?
Does the precept run 'Believe in good,
In justice, truth, now understood
For the first time?' — or, 'Believe in me,
Who lived and died, yet essentially
Am Lord of Life?' Whoever can take
The same to his heart and for mere love's sake
Conceive of the love, — that man obtains
A new truth; no conviction gains
Of an old one only, made intense
By a fresh appeal to his faded sense.

XVIII

Can it be that He stays inside?
   Is the Vesture left me to commune with?
     Could my soul find aught to sing in tune with
Even at this lecture, if she tried?
Oh, let me at lowest sympathize

With the lurking drop of blood that lies
In the desiccated brain's white roots
Without throb for Christ's attributes,
As the lecturer makes his special boast!
If love's dead there, it has left a ghost.
Admire we, how from heart to brain
   (Though to say so strike the doctors dumb)
One instinct rises and falls again,
   Restoring the equilibrium.
And how when the Critic had done his best,
And the pearl of price, at reason's test,
Lay dust and ashes levigable
On the Professor's lecture-table, —
When we looked for the inference and monition
That our faith, reduced to such condition,
Be swept forthwith to its natural dust-hole, —
   He bids us, when we least expect it,
Take back our faith, — if it be not just whole,
   Yet a pearl indeed, as his tests affect it,
Which fact pays damage done rewardingly,
So, prize we our dust and ashes accordingly!
'Go home and venerate the myth
I thus have experimented with —
This man, continue to adore him

Rather than all who went before him,
And all who ever followed after!' —
    Surely for this I may praise you, my brother!
Will you take the praise in tears or laughter?
    That's one point gained: can I compass another?
Unlearned love was safe from spurning —
Can't we respect your loveless learning?
Let us at least give learning honour!
What laurels had we showered upon her,
Girding her loins up to perturb
Our theory of the Middle Verb;
Or Turk-like brandishing a scimitar
O'er anapaests in comic-trimeter;
Or curing the halt and maimed 'Iketides',
While we lounged on at our indebted ease:
Instead of which, a tricksy demon
Sets her at Titus or Philemon!
When ignorance wags his ears of leather
And hates God's word, 'tis altogether;
Nor leaves he his congenial thistles
To go and browse on Paul's Epistles.
— And you, the audience, who might ravage
The world wide, enviably savage,
Nor heed the cry of the retriever,

More than Herr Heine (before his fever), —
I do not tell a lie so arrant
　　As say my passion's wings are furled up,
And, without plainest heavenly warrant,
　　I were ready and glad to give the world up —
But still, when you rub brow meticulous,
　　And ponder the profit of turning holy
　　If not for God's, for your own sake solely,
— God forbid I should find you ridiculous!
Deduce from this lecture all that eases you,
Nay, call yourselves, if the calling pleases you,
'Christians' — abhor the deist's pravity, —
Go on, you shall no more move my gravity
Than, when I see boys ride a-cockhorse,
I find it in my heart to embarrass them
By hinting that their stick's a mock horse,
And they really carry what they say carries them.

XIX

So sat I talking with my mind.
　　I did not long to leave the door
　　And find a new church, as before,
But rather was quiet and inclined
To prolong and enjoy the gentle resting

From further tracking and trying and testing.
This tolerance is a genial mood!
(Said I, and a little pause ensued.)
One trims the bark 'twixt shoal and shelf,
    And sees, each side, the good effects of it,
A value for religion's self,
    A carelessness about the sects of it.
Let me enjoy my own conviction,
    Not watch my neighbour's faith with fretfulness,
Still spying there some dereliction
    Of truth, perversity, forgetfulness!
Better a mild indifferentism,
    Teaching that both our faiths (though duller
His shine through a dull spirit's prism)
    Originally had one colour!
Better pursue a pilgrimage
    Through ancient and through modern times
    To many peoples, various climes,
Where I may see saint, savage, sage
Fuse their respective creeds in one
Before the general Father's throne!

— 'Twas the horrible storm began afresh!
The black night caught me in his mesh,
Whirled me up, and flung me prone.
I was left on the college-step alone.
I looked, and far there, ever fleeting
Far, far away, the receding gesture,
And looming of the lessening Vesture! —
Swept forward from my stupid hand,
While I watched my foolish heart expand
In the lazy glow of benevolence,

    O'er the various modes of man's belief.
I sprang up with fear's vehemence.

    Needs must there be one way, our chief
Best way of worship: let me strive
To find it, and when found, contrive
My fellows also take their share!
This constitutes my earthly care:
God's is above it and distinct.
For I, a man, with men am linked
And not a brute with brutes; no gain
That I experience, must remain
Unshared: but should my best endeavour
To share it, fail — subsisteth ever

God's care above, and I exult
That God, by God's own ways occult,
May — doth, I will believe — bring back
All wanderers to a single track.
Meantime, I can but testify
God's care for me — no more, can I —
It is but for myself I know;
    The world rolls witnessing around me
    Only to leave me as it found me;
Men cry there, but my ear is slow;
Their races flourish or decay
— What boots it, while yon lucid way
Loaded with stars divides the vault?
But soon my soul repairs its fault
When, sharpening sense's hebetude,
She turns on my own life! So viewed,
No mere mote's-breath but teems immense
With witnessings of providence:
And woe to me if when I look
Upon that record, the sole book
Unsealed to me, I take no heed
Of any warning that I read!
Have I been sure, this Christmas-Eve,
God's own hand did the rainbow weave,

Whereby the truth from heaven slid
Into my soul? — I cannot bid
The world admit He stooped to heal
My soul, as if in a thunder-peal
Where one heard noise, and one saw flame,
I only knew He named my name:
But what is the world to me, for sorrow
Or joy in its censure, when to-morrow
It drops the remark, with just-turned head
Then, on again, 'That man is dead'?
Yes, but for me — my name called, — drawn
As a conscript's lot from the lap's black yawn,
He has dipt into on a battle-dawn:
Bid out of life by a nod, a glance, —
Stumbling, mute-mazed, at nature's chance, —
With a rapid finger circled round,
Fixed to the first poor inch of ground
To fight from, where his foot was found;
Whose ear but a minute since lay free
To the wide camp's buzz and gossipry —
Summoned, a solitary man
To end his life where his life began,
From the safe glad rear, to the dreadful van!
Soul of mine, hadst thou caught and held
By the hem of the Vesture! —

    And I caught
At the flying robe, and unrepelled
Was lapped again in its folds full-fraught
With warmth and wonder and delight,
God's mercy being infinite.
For scarce had the words escaped my tongue,
When, at a passionate bound, I sprung,
Out of the wandering world of rain,
Into the little chapel again.

How else was I found there, bolt upright
    On my bench, as if I had never left it?
— Never flung out on the common at night,
    Nor met the storm and wedge-like cleft it,
Seen the raree-show of Peter's successor,
Or the laboratory of the Professor!
For the Vision, that was true, I wist,
True as that heaven and earth exist.
There sat my friend, and yellow and tall,
    With his neck and its wen in the selfsame place:
Yet my nearest neighbour's cheek showed gall.
    She had slid away a contemptuous space:

And the old fat woman, late so placable,
Eyed me with symptoms, hardly mistakable,
Of her milk of kindness turning rancid.
In short, a spectator might have fancied
That I had nodded, betrayed by slumber,
Yet kept my seat, a warning ghastly,
Through the heads of the sermon, nine in number,
And woke up now at the tenth and lastly.
But again, could such disgrace have happened?
    Each friend at my elbow had surely nudged it;
And, as for the sermon, where did my nap end?
    Unless I heard it, could I have judged it?
Could I report as I do at the close,
First, the preacher speaks through his nose:
Second, his gesture is too emphatic:
    Thirdly, to waive what's pedagogic,
    The subject-matter itself lacks logic:
Fourthly, the English is ungrammatic.
Great news! the preacher is found no Pascal,
Whom, if I please, I might to the task call
Of making square to a finite eye
    The circle of infinity,
And find so all-but-just-succeeding!
Great news! the sermon proves no reading

Where bee-like in the flowers I bury me,
Like Taylor's the immortal Jeremy!
And now that I know the very worst of him,
What was it I thought to obtain at first of him?
Ha! Is God mocked, as He asks?
Shall I take on me to change his tasks,
And dare, despatched to a river-head
    For a simple draught of the element,
Neglect the thing for which He sent,
    And return with another thing instead? —
Saying, 'Because the water found
Welling up from the underground,
Is mingled with the taints of earth,
While thou, I know, dost laugh at dearth,
And couldest, at wink or word, convulse
The world with the leap of a river-pulse, —
Therefore I turned from the oozings muddy,
    And bring Thee a chalice I found, instead:
See the brave veins in the breccia ruddy!
    One would suppose that the marble bled.
What matters the water? A hope I have nursed:
The waterless cup will quench my thirst.'
— Better have knelt at the poorest stream
    That trickles in pain from the straitest rift!

For the less or the more is all God's gift,
Who blocks up or breaks wide the granite-seam.
And here, is there water or not, to drink?

   I then, in ignorance and weakness,
Taking God's help, have attained to think
   My heart does best to receive in meekness
That mode of worship, as most to His mind,
Where earthly aids being cast behind,
His All in All appears serene
With the thinnest human veil between,
Letting the mystic lamps, the seven,
   The many motions of his spirit,
Pass, as they list, to earth from heaven.
   For the preacher's merit or demerit,
It were to be wished the flaws were fewer
   In the earthen vessel, holding treasure
Which lies as safe in a golden ewer;
   But the main thing is, does it hold good measure?
Heaven soon sets right all other matters! —
   Ask, else, these ruins of humanity,
This flesh worn out to rags and tatters,
   This soul at struggle with insanity,
Who thence take comfort — can I doubt? —
Which an empire gained, were a loss without.

May it be mine! And let us hope
That no worse blessing befall the Pope,
Turned sick at last of to-day's buffoonery,
 Of posturings and petticoatings,
 Beside his Bourbon bully's gloatings
In the bloody orgies of drunk poltroonery!
Nor may the Professor forego its peace
 At Göttingen presently, when, in the dusk
Of his life, if his cough, as I fear, should increase,
 Prophesied of by that horrible husk —
When thicker and thicker the darkness fills
The world through his misty spectacles,
And he gropes for something more substantial
 Than a fable, myth or personification, —
May Christ do for him what no mere man shall,
 And stand confessed as the God of salvation!
Meantime, in the still recurring fear
 Lest myself, at unawares, be found,
 While attacking the choice of my neighbours round,
With none of my own made — I choose here!
The giving out of the hymn reclaims me;
I have done : and if any blames me,
Thinking that merely to touch in brevity
 The topics I dwell on, were unlawful, —

Or worse, that I trench, with undue levity,
   On the bounds of the holy and the awful, —
I praise the heart, and pity the head of him,
And I refer myself to THEE, instead of him,
Who head and heart alike discernest,
   Looking below light speech we utter,
   When frothy spume and frequent sputter
Prove that the soul's depths boil in earnest!
May truth shine out, stand ever before us!
I put up pencil and join chorus
To Hepzibah Tune, without further apology,
   The last five verses of the third section
   Of the seventeenth hymn of Whitfield's Collection,
To conclude with the doxology.

Rabbi Ben Ezra

I

Grow old along with me!
The best is yet to be,
The last of life, for which the first was made:
Our times are in His hand
Who saith 'A whole I planned,
Youth shows but half; trust God: see all nor be afraid!'

II

Not that, amassing flowers,
Youth sighed 'Which rose make ours,
Which lily leave and then as best recall?'
Not that, admiring stars,
It yearned 'Nor Jove, nor Mars;
Mine be some figured flame which blends, transcends
                                        them all!'

III

Not for such hopes and fears
Annulling youth's brief years,
Do I remonstrate: folly wide the mark!
Rather I prize the doubt
Low kinds exist without,
Finished and finite clods, untroubled by a spark.

IV

Poor vaunt of life indeed,
Were man but formed to feed
On Joy, to solely seek and find and feast:
  Such feasting ended, then
  As sure an end to men;
Irks care the crop-full bird? Frets doubt the maw-crammed
                                                    beast?

V

Rejoice we are allied
To That which doth provide
And not partake, effect and not receive!
  A spark disturbs our clod;
  Nearer we hold of God
Who gives, than of His tribes that take, I must believe.

VI

Then, welcome each rebuff
That turns earth's smoothness rough,
Each sting that bids nor sit nor stand but go!
  Be our joys three-parts pain!
  Strive, and hold cheap the strain;
Learn, nor account the pang; dare, never grudge the throe!

99

For thence, — a paradox
Which comforts while it mocks, —
Shall life succeed in that it seems to fail:
What I aspired to be,
And was not, comforts me:
A brute I might have been, but would not sink i' the scale.

What is he but a brute
Whose flesh has soul to suit,
Whose spirit works lest arms and legs want play?
To man, propose this test —
Thy body at its best
How far can that project thy soul on its lone way?

Yet gifts should prove their use:
I own the Past profuse
Of power each side, perfection every turn:
Eyes, ears took in their dole,
Brain treasured up the whole;
Should not the heart beat once 'How good to live and
                                                    learn?'

X

Not once beat 'Praise be Thine!
  I see the whole design,
I, who saw power, see now love perfect too:
  Perfect I call Thy plan:
  Thanks that I was a man!
Maker, remake, complete, — I trust what Thou shalt do!'

XI

For pleasant is this flesh;
  Our soul, in its rose-mesh
Pulled ever to the earth, still yearns for rest;
  Would we some prize might hold
  To match those manifold
Possessions of the brute, — gain most, as we did best!

XII

Let us not always say
  'Spite of this flesh to-day
I strove, made head, gained ground upon the whole!'
  As the bird wings and sings,
  Let us cry 'All good things
Are ours, nor soul helps flesh more, now, than flesh helps
                                      soul!'

XIII

Therefore I summon age
To grant youth's heritage,
Life's struggle having so far reached its term:
Thence shall I pass, approved
A man, for aye removed
From the developed brute; a god though in the germ.

XIV

And I shall thereupon
Take rest, ere I be gone
Once more on my adventure brave and new:
Fearless and unperplexed,
When I wage battle next,
What weapons to select, what armour to indue.

XV

Youth ended, I shall try
My gain or loss thereby;
Leave the fire ashes, what survives is gold.
And I shall weigh the same,
Give life its praise or blame:
Young, all lay in dispute; I shall know, being old.

XVI

For note, when evening shuts,
  A certain moment cuts
The deed off, calls the glory from the grey:
  A whisper from the west
  Shoots — 'Add this to the rest,
Take it and try its worth: here dies another day.'

XVII

So, still within this life,
  Though lifted o'er its strife,
Let me discern, compare, pronounce at last,
  'This rage was right i' the main,
  That asquiescence vain:
The Future I may face now I have proved the Past.'

XVIII

For more is not reserved
  To man, with soul just nerved
To act to-morrow what he learns to-day:
  Here, work enough to watch
  The Master work, and catch
Hints of the proper craft, tricks of the tool's true play.

XIX

As it was better, youth
Should strive, through acts uncouth,
Toward making, than repose on aught found made:
So, better, age, exempt
From strife, should know, than tempt
Further. Thou waitedst age: wait death nor be afraid!

XX

Enough now, if the Right
And Good and Infinite
Be named here, as thou callest thy hand thine own,
With knowledge absolute,
Subject to no dispute
From fools that crowded youth, nor let thee feel alone.

XXI

Be there, for once and all,
Severed great minds from small,
Announced to each his station in the Past!
Was I, the world arraigned,
Were they, my soul disdained,
Right? Let age speak the truth and give us peace at last!

XXII

Now, who shall arbitrate?
Ten men love what I hate,
Shun what I follow, slight what I receive;
Ten, who in ears and eyes
Match me: we all surmise,
They this thing, and I that: whom shall my soul believe?

XXIII

Not on the vulgar mass
Called 'work', must sentence pass,
Things done, that took the eye and had the price;
O'er which, from level stand,
The low world laid its hand,
Found straightway to its mind, could value in a trice:

XXIV

But all, the world's coarse thumb
And finger failed to plumb,
So passed in making up the main account;
All instincts immature,
All purposes unsure,
That weighed not as his work, yet swelled the man's

amount:

Thoughts hardly to be packed
 Into a narrow act,
Fancies that broke through language and escaped;
 All I could never be,
 All, men ignored in me,
This, I was worth to God, whose wheel the pitcher shaped.

Ay, note that Potter's wheel.
 That metaphor! and feel
Why time spins fast, why passive lies our clay, —
 Thou, to whom fools propound,
 When the wine makes its round,
'Since life fleets, all is change; the Past gone, seize to-day!'

Fool! All that is, at all,
 Lasts ever, past recall;
Earth changes, but thy soul and God stand sure:
 What entered into thee,
 That was, is, and shall be:
Time's wheel runs back or stops: Potter and clay endure.

XXVIII

He fixed thee mid this dance
Of plastic circumstance,
This Present, thou, forsooth, wouldst fain arrest:
Machinery just meant
To give thy soul its bent,
Try thee and turn thee forth, sufficiently impressed.

XXIX

What though the earlier grooves
Which ran the laughing loves
Around thy base, no longer pause and press?
What though, about thy rim,
Skull-things in order grim
Grow out, in graver mood, obey the sterner stress?

XXX

Look not thou down but up!
To uses of a cup,
The festal board, lamp's flash and trumpet's peal,
The new wine's foaming flow,
The Master's lips a-glow!
Thou, heaven's consummate cup, what need'st thou with
earth's wheel?

XXXI

But I need, now as then,
Thee, God, who mouldest men;
And since, not even while the whirl was worst,
Did I, — to the wheel of life
With shapes and colours rife,
Bound dizzily, — mistake my end, to slake Thy thirst:

XXXII

So, take and use Thy work:
Amend what flaws may lurk,
What strain o' the stuff, what warpings past the aim!
My times be in Thy hand!
Perfect the cup as planned!
Let age approve of youth, and death complete the same!

Elizabeth Barrett Browning

To Flush, My Dog

I

Loving friend, the gift of one
Who her own true faith has run
    Through my lower nature,
Be my benediction said
With hand upon thy head,
    Gentle fellow-creature!

II

Like a lady's ringlets brown,
Flow thy silken ears adown
    Either side demurely
Of thy silver-suited breast
Shining out from all the rest
    Of thy body purely.

III

Darkly brown thy body is,
Till the sunshine striking this
    Alchemise its dulness,
When the sleek curls manifold
Flash all over into gold
    With a burnished fulness.

IV

Underneath my stroking hand,
Startled eyes of hazel bland
 Kindling, growing larger,
Up thou leapest with a spring,
Full of prank and curveting,
 Leaping like a charger.

V

Leap! thy broad tail waves a light,
Leap! thy slender feet are bright,
 Canopied in fringes;
Leap! those tasselled ears of thine
Flicker strangely, fair and fine
 Down their golden inches.

VI

Yet, my pretty, sportive friend,
Little is't to such an end
 That I praise thy rareness;
Other dogs may be thy peers
Haply in these drooping ears
 And this glossy fairness.

VII

But of thee it shall be said,
This dog watched beside a bed
  Day and night unweary,
Watched within a curtained room
Where no sunbeam brake the gloom
  Round the sick and dreary.

VIII

Roses, gathered for a vase,
In that chamber died apace,
  Beam and breeze resigning;
This dog only, waited on,
Knowing that when light is gone
  Love remains for shining.

IX

Other dogs in thymy dew
Tracked the hares and followed through
  Sunny moor or meadow;
This dog only, crept and crept
Next a languid cheek that slept,
  Sharing in the shadow.

Other dogs of loyal cheer
Bounded at the whistle clear,
  Up the woodside hieing;
This dog only, watched in reach
Of a faintly uttered speech
  Or a louder sighing.

And if one or two quick tears
Dropped upon his glossy ears
  Or a sigh came double,
Up he sprang in eager haste,
Fawning, fondling, breathing fast,
  In a tender trouble.

And this dog was satisfied
If a pale thin hand would glide
  Down his dewlaps sloping, —
Which he pushed his nose within,
After, — platforming his chin
  On the palm left open.

XIII

This dog, if a friendly voice
Call him now to blither choice
    Than such a chamber-keeping,
'Come out!' praying from the door, —
Presseth backward as before,
    Up against me leaping.

XIV

Therefore to this dog will I,
Tenderly not scornfully,
    Render praise and favour:
With my hand upon his head,
Is my benediction said
    Therefore and for ever.

XV

And because he loves me so,
Better than his kind will do
    Often man or woman,
Give I back more love again
Than dogs often take of men,
    Leaning from my Human.

XVI

Blessings on thee, dog of mine,
Pretty collars make thee fine.
    Sugared milk make fat thee!
Pleasures wag on in thy tail,
Hands of gentle motion fail
    Nevermore, to pat thee!

XVII

Downy pillow take thy head,
Silken coverlid bestead,
    Sunshine help thy sleeping!
No fly's buzzing wake thee up,
No man break thy purple cup
    Set for drinking deep in.

XVIII

Whiskered cats arointed flee,
Sturdy stoppers keep from thee
    Cologne distillations;
Nuts lie in thy path for stones,
And thy feast–day macaroons
    Turn to daily rations!

XIX

Mock I thee, in wishing weal? —
Tears are in my eyes to feel
  Thou are made so straitly,
Blessing needs must straiten too, —
Little canst thou joy or do,
  Thou who lovest greatly.

XX

Yet be blessèd to the height
Of all goods and all delight
  Pervious to thy nature;
Only loved beyond that line,
With a love that answers thine,
  Loving fellow-creature!

THE LOST BOWER

I

In the pleasant orchard-closes,
'God bless all our gains,' say we,
But 'May God bless all our losses'
Better suits with our degree.
Listen, gentle — ay, and simple! listen, children on the knee!

II

Green the land is where my daily
Steps in jocund childhood played,
Dimpled close with hill and valley,
Dappled very close with shade:
Summer-snow of apple-blossoms running up from glade to
glade.

III

There is one hill I see nearer
In my vision of the rest;
And a little wood seems clearer
As it climbeth from the west,
Sideway from the tree-locked valley, to the airy upland crest.

Small the wood is, green with hazels,
And, completing the ascent,
Where the wind blows and sun dazzles,
Thrills in leafy tremblement,
Like a heart that after climbing beateth quickly through
                                                    content.

Not a step the wood advances
O'er the open hill-top's bound;
There, in green arrest, the branches
See their image on the ground:
You may walk beneath them smiling, glad with sight and
                                                    glad with sound.

For you hearken on your right hand,
How the birds do leap and call
In the greenwood, out of sight and
Out of reach and fear of all;
And the squirrels crack the filberts through their cheerful
                                                    madrigal.

VII

On your left, the sheep are cropping
The slant grass and daisies pale,
And five apple-trees stand dropping
Separate shadows toward the vale
Over which, in choral silence, the hills look you their
'All hail!'

VIII

Far out, kindled by each other,
Shining hills on hills arise,
Close as brother leans to brother
When they press beneath the eyes
Of some father praying blessings from the gifts of paradise.

IX

While beyond, above them mounted,
And above their woods alsò,
Malvern hills, for mountains counted
Not unduly, loom a-row —
Keepers of Piers Plowman's visions through the
sunshine and the snow.

Yet, in childhood, little prized I
That fair walk and far survey;
'Twas a straight walk unadvised by
The least mischief worth a nay;
Up and down — as dull as grammar on the eve of holiday.

But the wood, all close and clenching
Bough in bough and root in root, —
No more sky (for overbranching)
At your head than at your foot, —
Oh, the wood drew me within it by a glamour past dispute!

Few and broken paths showed through it,
Where the sheep had tried to run, —
Forced with snowy wool to strew it
Round the thickets, when anon
They, with silly thorn-pricked noses, bleated back into
                                        the sun.

But my childish heart beat stronger
Than those thickets dared to grow:
I could pierce them! I could longer

Travel on, methought, than so:
Sheep for sheep-paths! braver children climb and creep
                              where they would go.

XIV

And the poets wander, said I,
Over places all as rude:
Bold Rinaldo's lovely lady
Sat to meet him in a wood:
Rosalinda, like a fountain, laughed out pure with solitude.

XV

And if Chaucer had not travelled
Through a forest by a well,
He had never dreamt nor marvelled
At those ladies fair and fell
Who lived smiling without loving in their island-citadel.

XVI

Thus I thought of the old singers
And took courage from their song,
Till my little struggling fingers
Tore asunder gyve and thong
Of the brambles which entrapped me, and the barrier
                              branches strong.

XVII

On a day, such pastime keeping,
    With a fawn's heart debonair,
Under-crawling, overleaping
    Thorns that prick and boughs that beat,
I stood suddenly astonied — I was gladdened unaware.

XVIII

From the place I stood in, floated
    Back the covert dim and close,
And the open ground was coated
    Carpet-smooth with grass and moss,
And the blue-bell's purple presence signed it worthily
                           across.

XIX

Here a linden-tree stood, bright'ning
    All adown its silver rind;
For as some trees draw the lightning,
    So this tree, unto my mind,
Drew to earth the blessèd sunshine from the sky where it
                           was shrined.

122

XX

Tall the linden-tree, and near it
An old hawthorn also grew;
And wood-ivy like a spirit
Hovered dimly round the two,
Shaping thence that bower of beauty which I sing of thus
to you.

XXI

'Twas a bower for garden fitter
Than for any woodland wide:
Though a fresh and dewy glitter
Struck it through from side to side,
Shaped and shaven was the freshness, as by garden–
cunning plied.

XXII

Oh, a lady might have come there,
Hooded fairly like her hawk,
With a book or lute in summer,
And a hope of sweeter talk, —
Listening less to her own music than for footsteps on the
walk!

XXIII

But that bower appeared a marvel
In the wildness of the place;
With such seeming art and travail,
Finely fixed and fitted was
Leaf to leaf, the dark-green ivy, to the summit from the
base.

XXIV

And the ivy veined and glossy
Was enwrought with eglantine:
And the wild hop fibred closely,
And the large-leaved columbine,
Arch of door and window-mullion, did right sylvanly
entwine.

XXV

Rose-trees either side the door were
Growing lithe and growing tall,
Each one set a summer warder
For the keeping of the hall, —
With a red rose and a white rose, leaning nodding at the
wall.

XXVI

As I entered, mosses hushing
Stole all noises from my foot;
And a green elastic cushion,
Clasped within the linden root,
Took me a chair of silence very rare and absolute.

XXVII

All the floor was paved with glory,
Greenly, silently inlaid
(Through quick motions made before me)
With fair counterparts in shade
Of the fair serrated ivy-leaves which slanted overhead.

XXVIII

'Is such pavement in a palace?'
So I questioned in my thought:
The sun, shining through the chalice
Of the red rose hung without,
Threw within a red libation, like an answer to my doubt.

XXIX

At the same time, on the linen
Of my childish lap there fell
Two white may-leaves, downward winning
Through the ceiling's miracle,
From a blossom, like and angel, out of sight yet blessing
                                          well.

XXX

Down to floor and up to ceiling
Quick I turned my childish face,
With an innocent appealing
For the secret of the place
To the trees, which surely knew it in partaking of the grace.

XXXI

Where's no foot of human creature
How could reach a human hand?
And if this be work of Nature,
Why has Nature turned so bland,
Breaking off from other wild-work? It was hard to
                                          understand.

XXXII

Was she weary of rough-doing,
Of the bramble and the thorn?
Did she pause in tender rueing
Here of all her sylvan scorn?
Or in mock of Art's deceiving was the sudden mildness
worn?

XXXIII

Or could this same bower (I fancied)
Be the work of Dryad strong,
Who surviving all that chancèd
In the world's old pagan wrong,
Lay hid, feeding in the woodland on the last true poet's
song?

XXXIV

Or was this the house of fairies,
Left, because of the rough ways,
Unassoiled by Ave Marys
Which the passing pilgrim prays,
And beyond St. Catherine's chiming on the blessèd
Sabbath days?

XXXV

So, young muser, I sat listening
To my fancy's wildest word:
On a sudden, through the glistening
Leaves around, a little stirred.
Came a sound, a sense of music which was rather felt than
heard.

XXXVI

Softly, finely, it inwound me;
From the world it shut me in, —
Like a fountain, falling round me,
Which with silver waters thin
Clips a little water Naiad sitting smilingly within.

XXXVII

Whence the music came, who knoweth?
I know nothing: but indeed
Pan or Faunus never bloweth
So much sweetness from a reed
Which has sucked the milk of waters at the oldest
river-head.

Never lark the sun can waken
With such sweetness! when the lark,
The high planets overtaking
In the half-evanished Dark,
Casts his singing to their singing, like an arrow to the mark.

Never nightingale so singeth:
Oh, she leans on thorny tree
And her poet-song she flingeth
Over pain to victory!
Yet she never sings such music, — or she sings it not to me.

Never blackbirds, never thrushes
Nor small finches sing as sweet,
When the sun strikes through the bushes
To their crimson clinging feet,
And their pretty eyes look sideways to the summer heavens
                                    complete.

XLI

If it were a bird, it seemèd
Most like Chaucer's, which, in sooth,
He of green and azure dreamèd,
While it sat in spirit-ruth
On that bier of a crowned lady, singing nigh her silent
                                            mouth.

XLII

If it were a bird? — ah, sceptic,
Give me 'yea' or give me 'nay' —
Though my soul were nympholeptic
As I heard that virèlay,
You may stoop your pride to pardon, for my sin is far away!

XLIII

I rose up in exaltation
And an inward trembling heat,
And (it seemed) in geste of passion
Dropped the music to my feet
Like a garment rustling downwards — such a silence
                                            followed it!

XLIV

Heart and head beat through the quiet
Full and heavily, though slower:
In the song, I think, and by it,
Mystic Presences of power
Had up-snatched me to the Timeless, then returned me to
the Hour.

XLV

In a child-abstraction lifted,
Straightway from the bower I past,
Foot and soul being dimly drifted
Through the greenwood, till, at last,
In the hill-top's open sunshine I all consciously was cast.

XLVI

Face to face with the true mountains
I stood silently and still,
Drawing strength from fancy's dauntings,
From the air about the hill,
And from Nature's open mercies and most debonair
goodwill.

XLVII

Oh, the golden-hearted daisies
Witnessed there, before my youth,
To the truth of things, with praises
Of the beauty of the truth;
And I woke to Nature's real, laughing joyfully for both.

XLVIII

And I said within me, laughing,
I have found a bower to-day,
A green lusus, fashioned half in
Chance and half in Nature's play,
And a little bird sings nigh it, I will nevermore missay.

XLIX

Henceforth, I will be the fairy
Of this bower not built by one;
I will go there, sad or merry,
With each morning's benison,
And the bird shall be my harper in the dreamhall I have
                                                              won.

L

So I said. But the next morning,
(— Child, look up into my face —
'Ware, oh sceptic, of your scorning!

132

This is truth in its pure grace!)
The next morning, all had vanished, or my wandering
missed the place.

LI

Bring an oath most sylvan-holy,
And upon it swear me true —
By the wind-bells swinging slowly
Their mute curfews in the dew,
By the advent of the snowdrop, by the rosemary and rue, —

LII

I affirm by all or any,
Let the cause be charm or chance,
That my wandering searches many
Missed the bower of my romance —
That I nevermore upon it turned my mortal countenance.

LIII

I affirm that, since I lost it,
Never bower has seemed so fair:
Never garden-creeper crossed it
With so deft and brave an air,
Never bird sung in the summer, as I saw and heard them
there.

LIV

Day by day, with new desire,
Toward my wood I ran in faith,
Under leaf and over brier,
Through the thickets, out of breath;
Like the prince who rescued Beauty from the sleep as long
as death.

LV

But his sword of mettle clashèd,
And his arm smote strong, I ween,
And her dreaming spirit flashèd
Through her body's fair white screen,
And the light therof might guide him up the cedar alleys
green:

LVI

But for me I saw no splendour —
All my sword was my child-heart;
And the wood refused surrender
Of that bower it held apart,
Safe as Œdipus's grave-place 'mid Colonos' olives swart.

LVII

As Aladdin sought the basements
His fair palace rose upon,
And the four-and-twenty casements

Which gave answers to the sun;
So, in 'wilderment of gazing, I looked up and I looked
down.

LVIII

Years have vanished since, as wholly
As the little bower did then;
And you call it tender folly
That such thoughts should come again?
Ah, I cannot change this sighing for your smiling, brother
men!

LIX

For this loss it did prefigure
Other loss of better good,
When my soul, in spirit-vigour
And in ripened womanhood,
Fell from visions of more beauty than an arbour in a wood.

LX

I have lost — oh, many a pleasure,
Many a hope and many a power —
Studious health and merry leisure,
The first dew on the first flower!
But the first of all my losses was the losing of the bower.

LXI

I have lost the dream of Doing,
And the other dream of Done,
The first spring in the pursuing,
The first pride in the Begun, —
First recoil from incompletion, in the face of what is won —

LXII

Exaltations in the far light
Where some cottage only is;
Mild dejections in the starlight,
Which the sadder-hearted miss;
And the child-cheek blushing scarlet for the very shame of
bliss.

LXIII

I have lost the sound child-sleeping
Which the thunder could not break;
Something too of the strong leaping
Of the staglike heart awake,
Which the pale is low for keeping in the road it ought to
take.

LXIV

Some respect to social fictions
Has been also lost by me;
And some generous genuflexions,
Which my spirit offered free
To the pleasant old conventions of our false humanity.

LXV

All my losses did I tell you,
Ye perchance would look away: —
Ye would answer me, 'Farewell! you
Make sad company to-day,
And your tears are falling faster than the bitter words you
say.'

LXVI

For God placed me like a dial
In the open ground with power,
And my heart had for its trial
All the sun and all the shower:
And I suffered many losses, — and my first was of the
bower.

LXVII

Laugh you? If that loss of mine be
Of no heavy-seeming weight —
When the cone falls from the pine-tree,
The young children laugh thereat;
Yet the wind that struck it, riseth, and the tempest shall be
*   great.*

LXVIII

One who knew me in my childhood
In the glamour and the game,
Looking on me long and mild, would
Never know me for the same.
Come, unchanging recollections, where those changes
*   overcame!*

LXIX

By this couch I weakly lie on,
While I count my memories, —
Through the fingers which, still sighing,
I press closely on mine eyes, —
Clear as once beneath the sunshine, I behold the bower
*   arise.*

138

LXX

Springs the linden-tree as greenly,
Stroked with light adown its rind;
And the ivy-leaves serenely
Each in either intertwined;
And the rose-trees at the doorway, they have neither grown
nor pined.

LXXI

From those overblown faint roses
Not a leaf appeareth shed,
And that little bud discloses
Not a thorn's breadth more of red,
For the winters and the summers which have passed me
overhead.

LXXII

And that music overfloweth,
Sudden sweet, the sylvan eaves:
Thrush or nightingale — who knoweth?
Fay or Faunus — who believes?
But my heart still trembles in me to the trembling of the
leaves.

Is the bower lost, then? who sayeth
That the bower indeed is lost?
Hark! my spirit in it prayeth
Through the sunshine and the frost, —
And the prayer preserves it greenly, to the last and
          uttermost.

Till another open for me
In God's Eden-land unknown,
With an angel at the doorway,
White with gazing at His Throne;
And a saint's voice in the palm-trees, singing — *'All is lost*
          . . . and won!'

CHANGE UPON CHANGE

I

Five months ago the stream did flow,
  The lilies bloomed within the sedge,
And we were lingering to and fro,
Where none will track thee in this snow,
  Along the stream beside the hedge.
Ah, Sweet, be free to love and go!
  For if I do not hear thy foot,
  The frozen river is as mute,
  The flowers have dried down to the root:
  And why, since these be changed since May,
    Shouldst thou change less than they?

II

And slow, slow as the winter snow
  The tears have drifted to mine eyes;
And my poor cheeks, five months ago
Set blushing at thy praises so,
  Put paleness on for a disguise.
Ah Sweet, be free to praise and go!
  For if my face is turned too pale,
  It was thine oath that first did fail, —
  It was thy love proved false and frail, —
  And why, since these be changed enow,
    Should I change less than thou?

SONNETS FROM THE PORTUGUESE (1847–1850)

XIII

And wilt thou have me fashion into speech
The love I bear thee, finding words enough,
And hold the torch out, while the winds are rough,
Between our faces, to cast light on each? —
I drop it at thy feet. I cannot teach
My hand to hold my spirit so far off
From myself — me — that I should bring thee proof
In words, of love hid in me out of reach.
Nay, let the silence of my womanhood
Commend my woman-love to thy belief, —
Seeing that I stand unwon, however wooed,
And rend the garment of my life, in brief,
By a most dauntless, voiceless fortitude,
Lest one touch of this heart convey its grief.

XIV

If thou must love me, let it be for nought
Except for love's sake only. Do not say
'I love her for her smile — her look — her way
Of speaking gently, — for a trick of thought
That falls in well with mine, and certes brought

A sense of pleasant ease on such a day' —
For these things in themselves, Beloved, may
Be changed, or change for thee, — and love, so wrought,
May be unwrought so. Neither love me for
Thine own dear pity's wiping my cheeks dry, —
A creature might forget to weep, who bore
Thy comfort long, and lose thy love thereby!
But love me for love's sake, that evermore
Thou mayst love on, through love's eternity.

XXIX

I think of thee! — my thoughts do twine and bud
About thee, as wild vines, about a tree,
Put out broad leaves, and soon there's nought to see
Except the straggling green which hides the wood.
Yet, O my palm-tree, be it understood
I will not have my thoughts instead of thee
Who art dearer, better! Rather, instantly
Renew thy presence; as a strong tree should,
Rustle thy boughs and set thy trunk all bare,
And let these bands of greenery which insphere thee
Drop heavily down, — burst, shattered, everywhere!
Because, in this deep joy to see and hear thee

And breathe within thy shadow a new air,
I do not think of thee — I am too near thee.

XXXVII

Pardon, oh, pardon, that my soul should make,
Of all that strong divineness which I know
For thine and thee, an image only so
Formed of the sand, and fit to shift and break.
It is that distant years which did not take
Thy sovranty, recoiling with a blow,
Have forced my swimming brain to undergo
Their doubt and dread, and blindly to forsake
Thy purity of likeness and distort
Thy worthiest love to a worthless conterfeit:
As if a shipwrecked Pagan, safe in port,
His guardian sea-god to commemorate,
Should set a sculptured porpoise, gills a-snort
And vibrant tail, within the temple-gate.